Investigating the Chemistry
of Atoms

Elizabeth R. C. Cregan, MDE

Physical Science Readers:
Investigating the Chemistry of Atoms

Publishing Credits

Editorial Director
Dona Herweck Rice

Creative Director
Lee Aucoin

Associate Editor
Joshua BishopRoby

Illustration Manager
Timothy J. Bradley

Editor-in-Chief
Sharon Coan, M.S.Ed.

Publisher
Rachelle Cracchiolo, M.S.Ed.

Science Contributor
Sally Ride Science

Science Consultant
Jane Weir, MPhys

Teacher Created Materials
5301 Oceanus Drive
Huntington Beach, CA 92649-1030
http://www.tcmpub.com
ISBN 978-0-7439-0569-5
© 2007 Teacher Created Materials, Inc.

Table of Contents

This book has something important in common with the breakfast you ate this morning. Your breakfast has something in common with your hands holding this book. In fact, everything around you has it in common. Can you guess what it is?

All things are made of **matter**. Matter makes up everything. Scientists say that matter is anything that takes up space. Even if the space is too small to see, matter is still there.

But what is matter made of? No matter what, matter is made of tiny **particles**. They are called **atoms**. Atoms are the building blocks of everything. They are everywhere. They are the air you breathe. They are the food you eat, the things you touch, and the clothes you wear. They are every part of you.

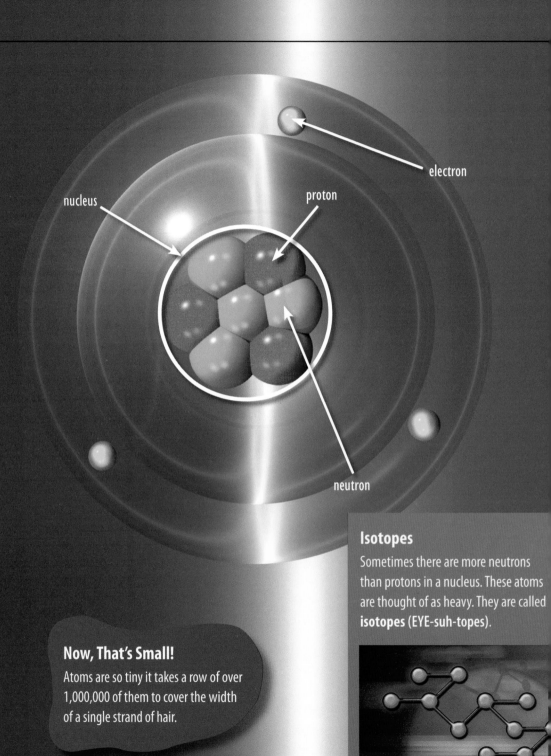

electron

nucleus

proton

neutron

Isotopes

Sometimes there are more neutrons than protons in a nucleus. These atoms are thought of as heavy. They are called **isotopes** (EYE-suh-topes).

Now, That's Small!

Atoms are so tiny it takes a row of over 1,000,000 of them to cover the width of a single strand of hair.

If you could peek inside an atom, you would see a lot going on. First you might notice its small, tightly packed center. This is called the **nucleus** (NOO-klee-uhs). Inside the nucleus are even tinier particles. They are called **protons** (PROH-tons) and **neutrons** (NOO-trons). There are usually the same number of protons and neutrons in an atom. Squeezed tightly together, they form the nucleus.

Look again, and you will see clouds of particles called **electrons** (uh-LEK-trons). They orbit around the nucleus. The same number of electrons and protons are in each atom.

Protons and electrons each have an electric charge. In protons, the charge is positive. In electrons, the charge is negative. Together, they balance the atom's charge. The atom as a whole is neither positive nor negative.

▼ Students in a lab build a model of an atom.

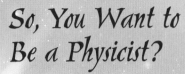

So, You Want to Be a Physicist?

If you're very curious and creative, physics might be the field for you. Physics is the science that studies energy and matter and how they interact. These scientists try to answer big and small questions about the universe. What are stars made of? What makes the tides go in and out? Most physicists do research to try to answer these questions. They teach and write about their experiments. Margaret Burbidge is one such scientist. She studies the stars. Her research has shown how heavier elements can be built from lighter ones inside of stars. Her work is definitely out of this world!

For a long time, scientists thought they knew all the parts of an atom. Then they learned that there is more. Protons and neutrons are made of something even smaller. They are tiny particles called **quarks** (kwarks). Quarks are the smallest parts of an atom.

Scientists have worked for more than 2,000 years to learn what we know about atoms. Everything they have learned is part of the **Atomic Theory**. The story begins in Ancient Greece. It continues even today.

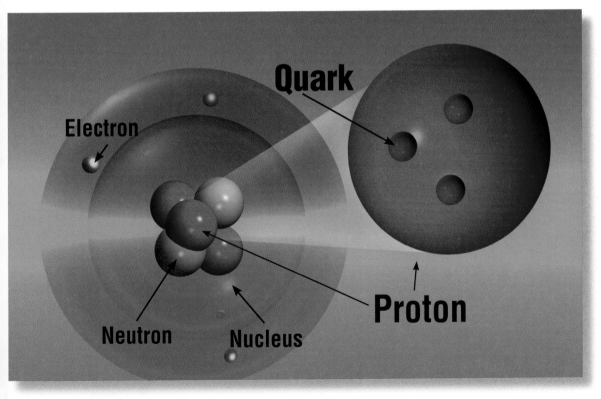

This diagram shows that while protons and neutrons are tiny parts of an atom, quarks are even smaller.

Old and New

Ancient Greek philosophers like Democritus and Aristotle watched the world around them. Many thought that all matter was made of four **elements**. They were air, fire, water, and earth.

Democritus wondered something. Is it possible to break matter into smaller pieces? And can you keep breaking the pieces forever? He decided the answer is no. At some point, there would be a pile of tiny bits that could no longer be broken. He named the bits *atomos*. It means "unbreakable."

▲ Statue of Democritus

▲ Statue of Aristotle

Air

Earth

Water

Fire

Aristotle also thought that matter was made of the four elements. He added a fifth element called ether, which he believed filled up outer space. He thought that one element could be changed into another.

Scientists started to try out this idea. They began a branch of science called **alchemy** (AL-kuh-mee). They tried to change metals, such as lead, into gold and silver. For hundreds of years, people believed the ideas of Aristotle and the alchemists.

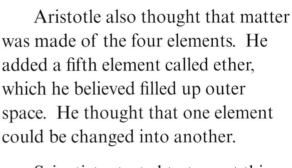

Strange But True

Although the alchemists never figured out how to turn lead into gold, they did discover a new element. One person thought he could turn urine into gold because they were the same color. His work led to the discovery of the element phosphorous. Phosphorous is used on the tips of matches.

John Dalton, Founder of Modern Atomic Theory

Alchemy was used for hundreds of years. No one thought much about the old idea of atoms. Then along came John Dalton in 1804. Dalton was an English scientist. He took another look at the old Greek idea. He thought it was true. Matter really is made of atoms.

He said there are many different kinds of atoms. Groups of one kind of atom make up an element. All the atoms of an element are the same. Each atom in an element has the same number of protons, neutrons, and electrons. It also has the same **mass**. This mass is also called its **atomic** (uh-TOM-ik) **weight.**

Dalton thought you could tell atoms apart by their atomic weights. He also thought that atoms were the most basic matter. He didn't think they could be divided any further.

Scientists still had questions. Why are elements different? What makes them different? Is it possible to look inside an atom? They would soon discover that atoms are breakable. The alchemists weren't all wrong. It is possible to change elements. By

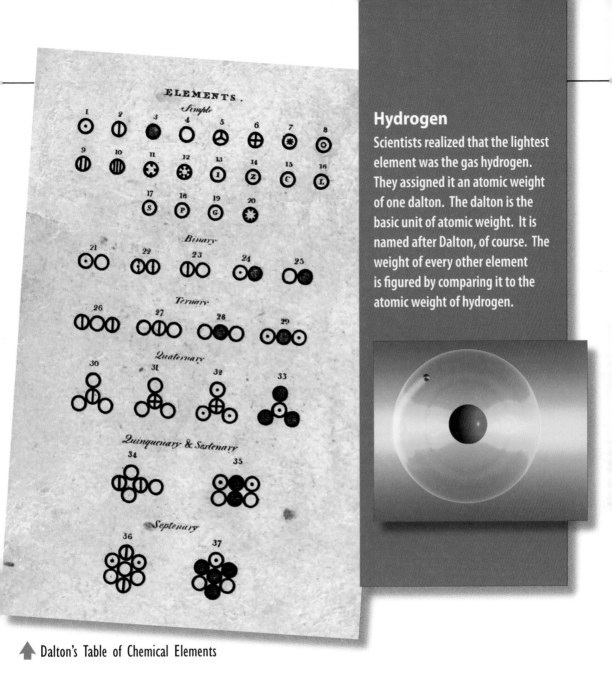

Dalton's Table of Chemical Elements

the late 1800s, many scientists used **electricity**. It helped them to break down substances into their elements. Scientists could find each element's atomic weight. This helped them to find many new elements.

Cathode Rays and Electrons

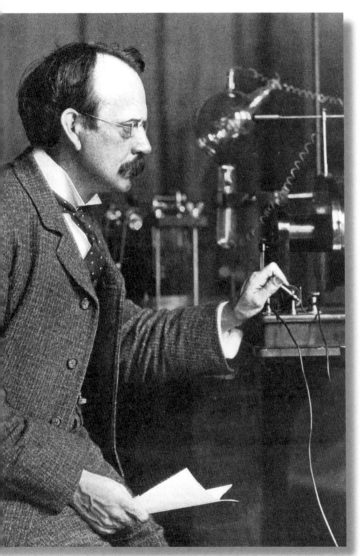

🔺 J. J. Thomson first studied cathode rays.

In 1897, an English scientist named Joseph John Thomson studied a special glow of energy. It came from an electric current run through a glass tube. The tube was empty of all air and gases. This emptiness is called a **vacuum**. The glow Thomson saw was energy. He called it **cathode** (KATH-ohd) **rays.**

German scientists believed this glow was made by Aristotle's ether. French and English scientists thought it was caused by some kind of particle that glowed when hit by electricity. Thomson proved that cathode rays were made of particles. He named the particles corpuscles (KORE-puh-suhls).

Thomson believed that all atoms had corpuscles. He also thought that each corpuscle was much smaller than its atom. Corpuscles later became known as electrons.

Cathode ray tubes

Do You Know the Muffin Man?

Thomson created the Blueberry Muffin Model of the atom. He believed the atom was a sphere of spongy material with a positive charge. Electrons, which have a negative charge, sat in the spongy material like blueberries in a muffin. It was also called the Plum Pudding Model. This model was later disproved.

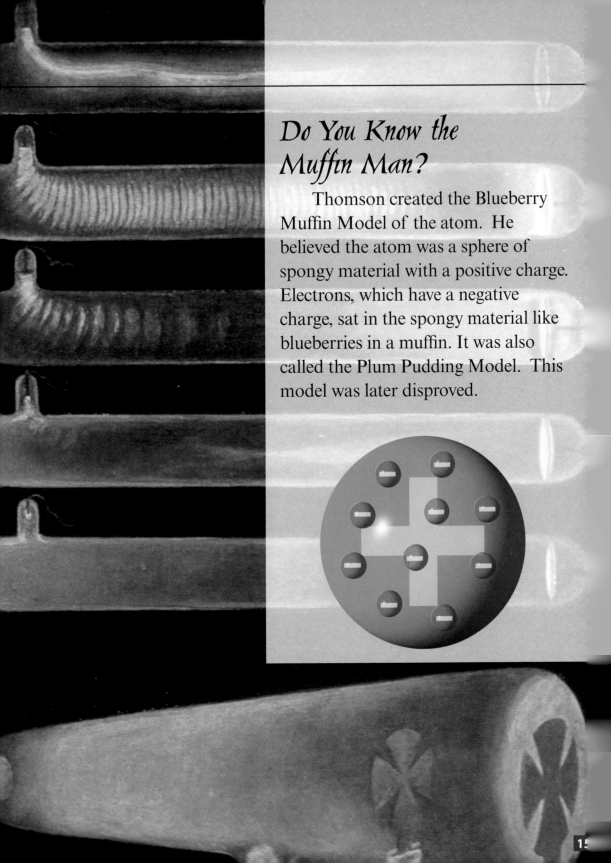

Radioactivity

Thomson learned that corpuscles could expose film to take pictures. It could even expose film when the tube was wrapped in black cloth. Other scientists studied the same glow that Thomson did. They called this energy source **X-rays**.

Scientists were curious about X-rays. One found that the element **uranium** (yoo-RAY-nee-uhm) made energy even stronger than X-rays. Most scientists ignored this. But a Polish scientist named Marie Curie didn't. She wanted to learn more about uranium and its energy. She and her husband Pierre tested many elements. They found several that made this energy. They named the energy **radioactivity**.

The Curies wondered where the energy came from. Something was happening inside the atom. It held many mysteries.

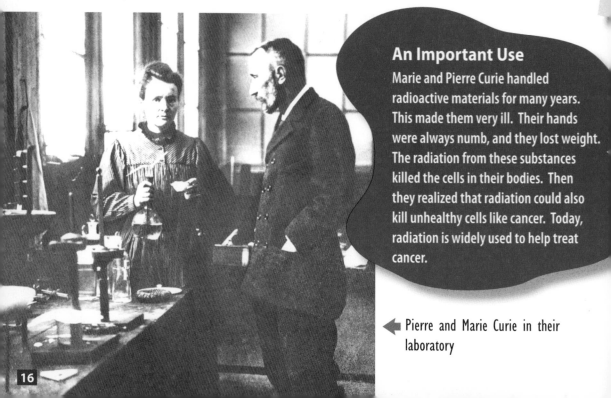

An Important Use

Marie and Pierre Curie handled radioactive materials for many years. This made them very ill. Their hands were always numb, and they lost weight. The radiation from these substances killed the cells in their bodies. Then they realized that radiation could also kill unhealthy cells like cancer. Today, radiation is widely used to help treat cancer.

Pierre and Marie Curie in their laboratory

Radium Girls

Before scientists realized the dangers of handling **radium**, people used it for all kinds of things. There was radium butter and radium toothpaste. A paint made with radium was used on watches and airplane instruments to make them glow in the dark. Women known as "Radium Girls" worked in factories, using the radium paint. Just for fun, they painted their teeth to make them glow in the dark. The Radium Girls became very sick and died of cancer.

Chauffage

We solicit your close inspection and guarantee
Radium Brand Butter
To please the most delicate appetite

Radium Brand
CREAMERY BUTTER

ONE POUND NET
Radium Brand Butter

⬆ Everyday products commonly contained dangerous amounts of radium before scientists knew the health risks.

The Work of Ernest Rutherford

Ernest Rutherford worked as Joseph Thomson's assistant. His work built upon Thomson's work. Rutherford was interested in X-rays and radioactivity. He studied the element uranium. He exposed it to a strong magnetic field. In this way, he found that it threw off particles to make radiation. He thought the atoms must be made of lots of these small particles.

Ernest Rutherford

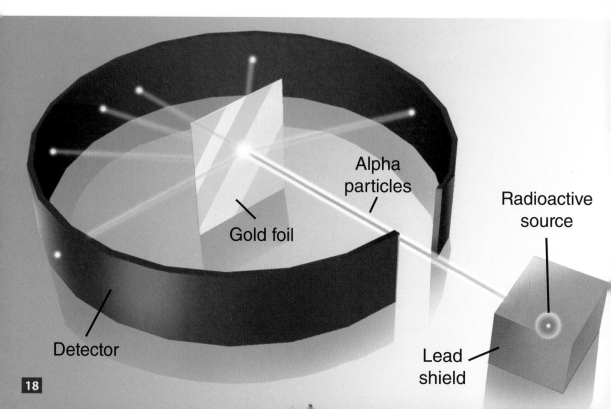

Alpha particles

Radioactive source

Gold foil

Detector

Lead shield

The Alchemists Weren't All Wrong

It's hard to imagine that people really believed it was possible to turn a metal like lead into gold or silver. Scientists worked for centuries trying to do just that. Along the way, they found some new elements. But no one ever turned lead into gold. As it turns out, they had the right idea. It was just backwards. Today, we know that radioactive elements such as radium decay and turn into lead. It just takes a little time—almost 20,000 years!

Rutherford used the Gold Foil Experiment to prove it. He shot radiation through a thin piece of gold foil. His results made him believe that the atom has a tightly packed center with other particles going around it.

If he was right, Rutherford would prove that the Blueberry Muffin Model was wrong. The blueberries were flying around the muffin, not sitting inside it. He also thought that there might be a particle with no charge in the atom. Another scientist found the particle. It was the neutron.

Atomic Comics

Work with radioactivity had a big effect on the entire world. Comic books like **Radioactive Man, Atomic Mouse, Atomic Rabbit, Inside the Atom, Reacto Man,** and **Atomic Superboy** were very popular in the 1950s and 1960s. Some were written to explain atomic energy and the use of electricity. Others told fantastic stories where radiation turned regular people into superheroes.

The Work of Iréne Joliot-Curie

Iréne Joliot-Curie was the daughter of Marie Curie. She was her mother's assistant. Joliot-Curie and her husband studied the **radioactive decay** of elements. They searched for ways to make radioactive substances in the lab. They found that some substances decay in seconds. Others take millions of years to decay.

Their work led to the discovery of **fission** (FISH-uhn). Fission is splitting apart the nucleus of an atom. For a very long time, scientists thought an atom could not be split. It is possible, just very hard to do. The split creates large amounts of energy.

Joliot-Curie and her husband shared the Nobel Prize in chemistry in 1935. Twenty years later, she died of cancer, just as her mother had. Working with radioactive materials caused their illnesses.

⬇ How nuclear fission works

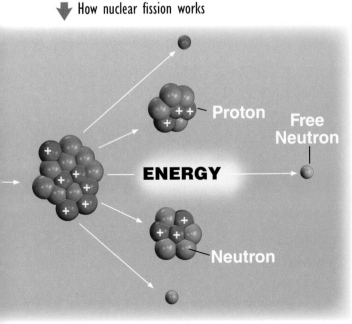

⬇ Iréne Joliot-Curie

21

A New Model

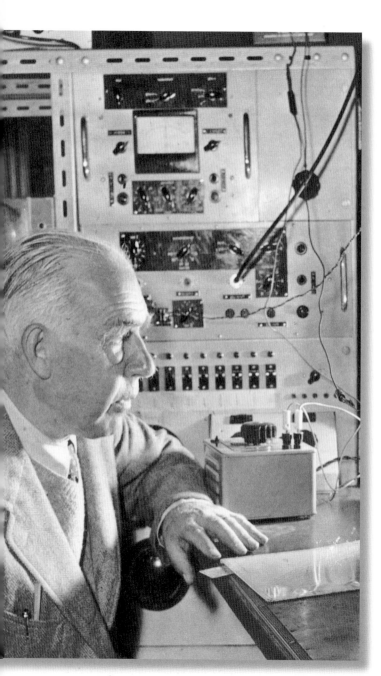

In 1913, a scientist named Niels Bohr worked with Rutherford's ideas. He made a new model of the atom. Bohr's Model says that atoms are made of three kinds of particles. They are protons, neutrons, and electrons. There are about the same number of protons and neutrons in an atom. There are exactly the same number of protons and electrons. The nucleus of the atom is a tightly packed center. It has protons and neutrons. Electrons orbit the nucleus like planets orbit the sun. They whiz through the empty space around the nucleus.

Later, Bohr changed his mind about electrons circling the nucleus in this way. He thought the orbits were more like energy

▲ Niels Bohr

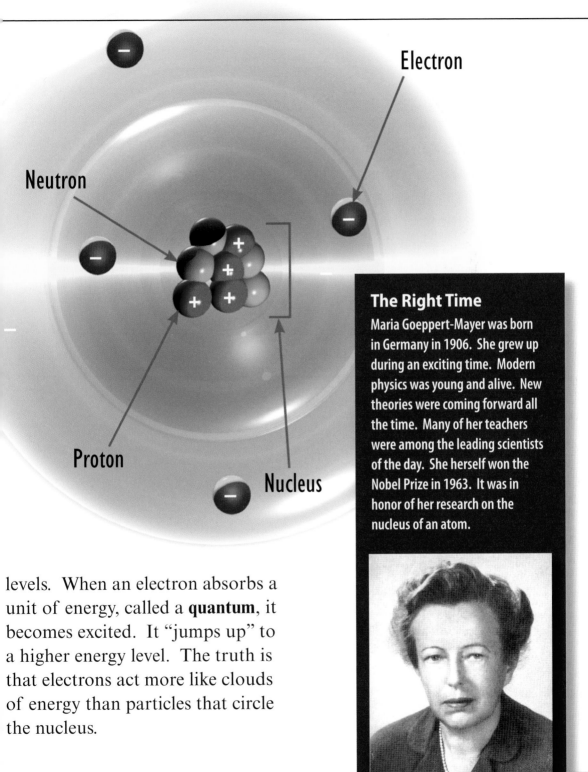

Electron

Neutron

Proton

Nucleus

levels. When an electron absorbs a unit of energy, called a **quantum**, it becomes excited. It "jumps up" to a higher energy level. The truth is that electrons act more like clouds of energy than particles that circle the nucleus.

Atom Smashers

Particle accelerators are also called atom smashers because that's what they do. They smash electrons into atoms. This releases energy particles for scientists to study.

An atom smasher covers acres of land. To see it all, you'd need to take a helicopter ride! Physicists use atom smashers to search for the tiniest building blocks of matter. In an atom smasher, an electromagnet moves a beam of electrons down a copper tube. The tube can be as long as three kilometers (two miles) long. When they reach the end, the electrons smash into a target. Subatomic particles like quarks and radiation are released.

Particle accelerator

The Particle Zoo

The more scientists studied the atom, the more complicated it seemed. They finally realized there was much more to atoms than they thought. They used machines called **particle accelerators** (ak-SEL-uh-ray-ters), or atom smashers. The machines helped them find many new **subatomic particles**. Subatomic means smaller than an atom or part of an atom.

In 1963, a scientist named Murray Gell-Mann thought that all subatomic particles were made of even tinier particles. He called these "quarks." He picked the name quark from one of his favorite books. He found six different types of them. He called them up, down, charm, strange, top, and bottom. Gell-Mann was only joking when he named the types of quarks. But somehow the names stuck!

Atom smashers have helped to find hundreds of subatomic particles. There are so many that scientists call them the particle zoo.

▲ Murray Gell-Mann

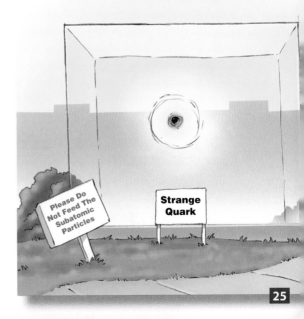

Please Do Not Feed The Subatomic Particles

Strange Quark

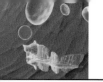

The Future

Scientists continue to build more powerful atom smashers. They help scientists find new subatomic particles. Scientists aren't sure that the quark is nature's most basic unit. There may always be questions about atoms that scientists can't answer. They have learned enough to put Atomic Theory to good use.

Atomic Theory has let scientists develop many things. We now have X-rays, cancer treatments, atomic energy, artificial elements, new drugs, and atomic weapons.

Scientists keep learning more about the atom. They create new ways to use the information. Who knows what the future will hold?

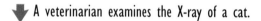

A veterinarian examines the X-ray of a cat.

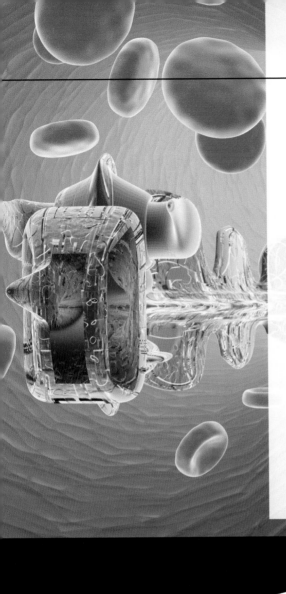

A Robot You Can Swallow

Imagine swallowing a robot so tiny it would take a microscope to see it. Scientists are working on ways to build very tiny objects called nanorobots. Nanorobots are built by arranging atoms one at a time. In the future, it may be possible to program nanorobots to find cells in the human body that cause illnesses like cancer. These nanorobots would destroy the cancer cells and leave the healthy cells alone. Doctors may even be able to send messages to nanorobots with sound waves to check how many cells they have destroyed.

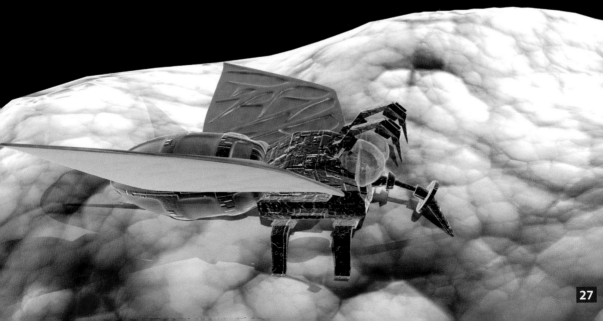

Lab: *Indirect Evidence*

Pioneers in atomic science often had to work with things that they could not see or touch themselves. They couldn't see atoms one at a time. Instead, they had to use indirect evidence. Indirect evidence is when you observe the effects of something. Then you make conclusions about the thing itself. It's like studying footprints in the mud to figure out who walked through the garden.

Materials

- empty boxes, labeled with letters or colors
- a collection of ordinary classroom or household items
- scale
- table

Procedure

1   Ask someone else to prepare a number of mystery boxes. If you are doing this experiment in school, your teacher will prepare the boxes. In each mystery box there should be one or more items from your classroom or home.

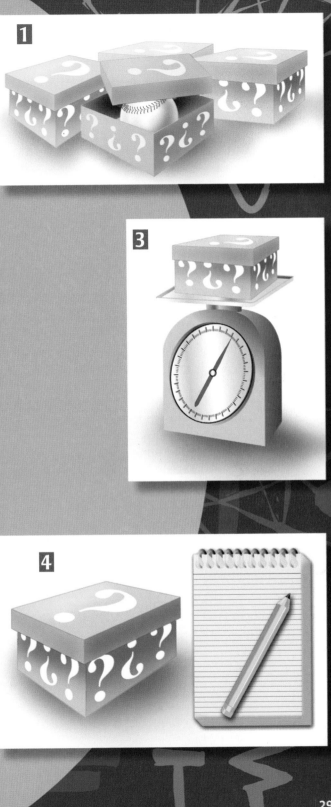

2 On a table, set out a number of items including those that have been placed in the mystery boxes. In this way, the items in the boxes will have a match somewhere on the table.

3 Without opening the mystery boxes, try to figure out what is inside each one. You can use your senses as well as any scientific instruments, such as a scale, you have available.

4 Record your hypothesis and the reasons for your hypothesis for each mystery box.

Glossary

alchemy—the science of changing metals such as lead into gold and silver

atom—the smallest particle of an element

Atomic Theory—a theory that proposes that matter is made up of atoms

atomic weight—the amount of matter contained in a single atom

cathode rays—beams of electrons

electricity—a form of energy made up of a stream of electrons

electron—small particles with negative charge that travel fast around an atom

element—one of nature's most basic substances, made up of a single kind of atom

fission—the splitting apart of the nucleus of an atom to create large amounts of energy

isotope—different forms of an element in which the atoms have more neutrons

mass—the amount of matter something has

matter—the substance of which everything is made

nucleus—an atom's dense center containing protons and neutrons

neutron—the particle found in the nucleus of an atom with a neutral electrical charge

particle—a very small piece

particle accelerator—machines that help scientists identify new subatomic particles

proton—the particle found in the nucleus of an atom with a positive electrical charge

quantum—unit of energy

quark—subatomic particles that form protons and neutrons

radioactive decay—the breakdown of radioactive substances as nuclei break apart

radioactivity—the process of giving off energy as a substance's atoms break apart

radium—a highly radioactive metallic element

subatomic particles—pieces smaller than and part of an atom

uranium—a radioactive element found in pitchblende

vacuum—an empty space containing no matter

X-rays—powerful images taken with cathode rays

Index

Sally Ride Science

Sally Ride Science™ is an innovative content company dedicated to fueling young people's interests in science. Our publications and programs provide opportunities for students and teachers to explore the captivating world of science—from astrobiology to zoology. We bring science to life and show young people that science is creative, collaborative, fascinating, and fun.

Image Credits

Cover Nemanja Glumac/Shutterstock; p.3 Jean-Loup Charmet/Photo Researchers, Inc.; p.4 (top) Dragan Trifunovic/Shutterstock; p.4 (bottom) Hemera; p.4–5 (back) Songmi/Shutterstock; p.5 Danny E. Hooks/Shutterstock; p.5 Mike Allgood/Shutterstock; p.5 Carlos E. Santa Maria/Shutterstock; p.5 (right) Olga Shelego/Shutterstock; p.6 (back) Tim Bradley; p.6 (front) Photos.com; p.7 Photos.com; p.8 (back) Kirsty Pargeter/Shutterstock; p.8 (front) Fox Photos/Getty Images; p.9 Tim Bradley; p.10 (top) Antonio Jorge Nunes/Shutterstock; p.10 (right) Dhoxax/Shutterstock; p.10 (left) Haydn Hansell/Alamy; p.10–11 (back) Photos.com; p.10–11 (front) Photos.com; p.11 (right) Photos.com; p.12 The Granger Collection, New York; p.13 (left) The Granger Collection, New York; p.13 (right) Tim Bradley; p.14 (top) Photos.com; p.14 (bottom) Mary Evans/Photo Researchers, Inc.; p.15 Jean-Loup Charmet/Photo Researchers, Inc.; p.15 (right) Tim Bradley; p.16 (top) Tim Bradley; p.16 (bottom) The Granger Collection, New York; p.17 (bottom) Tim Bradley; p.17 (top) Mary Evans Picture Library/Alamy; p.18 (top) Christa DeRidder/Shutterstock; p.18 (bottom) Tim Bradley; p.18 (right) Library of Congress; p.19 Visual Arts Library (London)/Alamy; p.20 (top) Lesley Palmer; p.20 (bottom) Robert Dale/Getty Images; p.21 (left) Tim Bradley; p.21 (right) The Granger Collection, New York; p.22 (top) Tim Bradley; p.22 (bottom) The Granger Collection, New York; p.23 (left) Tim Bradley; p.23 (right) The Granger Collection, New York; p.24 Fermilab/Photo Researchers, Inc.; p.25 (top) ESTATE OF FRANCIS BELLO/Photo Researchers, Inc.; p.25 (bottom) Tim Bradley; p.26 (top) Christian Darkin/Shutterstock; p.26 (bottom) Mark William Penny/Shutterstock; p.27 (top) Christian Darkin/Shutterstock; p.27 (bottom) Christian Darkin/Shutterstock; p.28 (top) Mike Allgood/Shutterstock; p.28–29 Nicoll Rager Fuller; p.32 Getty Images

Investigating the Chemistry
of Atoms

Atoms are the building blocks of everything around us. Inside the atom is the nucleus, with protons and neutrons. But there are even smaller particles that make up protons and neutrons, called quarks. Everything that scientists know about atoms is part of atomic theory, which originated in ancient Greece, but continues even today.

Physical Science

TCM 10569

ISBN 978-0-7439-0569-5
50000

9 780743 905695

Digestion and Using Food

Wendy Conklin